Contents

King James I 2

Guy Fawkes 7

The Gunpowder Plot 12

Robert Catesby 16

Who goes on the bonfire? 20

What do you think? 22

Index 24

King James I

Four hundred years ago, a group of men tried to kill the King of England.

The king was King James the First.

They wanted to blow him up when he went to open the Houses of Parliament.

They took 36 barrels of gunpowder into the cellars under the Houses of Parliament.

The explosion would also kill a lot of other people.

Guy Fawkes

The man who was going to light the gunpowder was called Guy Fawkes.

But somebody found out what was happening. He told one of the king's friends.

The king's soldiers were sent to search the cellars and they found Guy Fawkes hiding there. They captured him.

When the people who lived in London heard about this, they lit bonfires in the streets.

They did this to show the king that they were happy that he had not been killed. They were glad that Guy Fawkes had been captured. The date was 5th November, 1605.

The Gunpowder Plot

We call what happened "The Gunpowder Plot". We remember it every year by setting off fireworks and lighting bonfires on 5th November.

We put a model of Guy Fawkes on our bonfires and watch it burn.

But are we burning the right person on top of our bonfires?

Guy Fawkes was not working on his own. There were 14 people in The Gunpowder Plot.

Robert Catesby

The plot was started by a man called Robert Catesby. It was his idea to kill the king.

Robert Catesby got other people who did not like the king to join him. Guy Fawkes was one of the last people to join.

They decided that Guy Fawkes was the best person to set off the explosion. Guy Fawkes had been a soldier and knew a lot about using gunpowder.

When Guy Fawkes was captured, the king's soldiers tried to make him tell them the names of the other men. Then they killed him.

Robert Catesby ran away from London as fast as he could, but soldiers chased him. They caught him and shot him.

Who goes on the bonfire?

So who should we put on top of the bonfire every year?

Should it be Guy Fawkes? He was going to set off the gunpowder and blow up the king.

Should it be Robert Catesby? He started The Gunpowder Plot. It was his idea to kill the king.

What do you think?

Should we burn "The Guy" or "The Robert"?

Index

barrels of gunpowder **5**

bonfires **10, 12, 13, 14, 20**

Catesby, Robert **16, 19, 21**

cellars **5, 9**

explosion **6, 17**

Fawkes, Guy **7, 9, 11, 13, 15, 16, 17, 18, 20**

fireworks **12**

gunpowder **5, 7, 17, 20**

Gunpowder Plot, The **12, 15, 21**

Houses of Parliament **4, 5**

James I, King of England **2, 3**